Drawing
and Selling
Cartoons

by Jack Markow

REVISED EDITION

Pitman Publishing Corporation

NEW YORK   TORONTO   LONDON

THE NEW YORKER

Contents

INTRODUCTION	3
Using a Sketch Book	3
Your Model	3
CREATING A CARTOON STYLE	4
The Features	5
Constructing a Complete Head	6
Pantomime Cartoon	7
Head Accessories	8
Constructing a Complete Figure	10
Hands	12
Feet	12
DRAWING CARTOON TYPES	13
Head Shapes	14
Girls	15
Animals	18
EMOTION	20
ACTION AND COMPOSTION	24
Violent Action	25
DRAWING BACKGROUNDS	28
Interiors	28
Outdoors	30
TECHNIQUE	30
Line Reproduction	31

Wash Half-tone	32
Rubbed Tone	33
CREATING CARTOON IDEAS	34
Surprise Ending Picture	34
Surprise Ending Caption	35
Reverse Gag	35
Cliché Picture	36
Cliché Caption	37
The Gadget Gag	37
Gags Based on Signs	38
General Subjects	39
FROM ROUGH TO FINISH	40
Preparing the Rough	40
The Caption	41
The Finished Cartoon	42
The OK	42
SELLING	43
Which Magazine	43
When to Show	44
Selling by Mail	44
Related Fields	44
Caricature	45
Humorous Illustration	45
Comic Strips and Panels	45
Cartoon Spots	45
Greeting Cards	46

Introduction

This book is primarily for the would-be cartoonist, amateur or professional. Some may want to cartoon for fun; others, such as salesmen and other businessmen, may desire a knowledge of cartooning as a visual aid in talks and lectures. For the nonprofessional, just a few pointers picked up in this book are sufficient. For those of you who want to make cartooning your profession, close study and constant application of the methods described in this book are necessary, complemented by detailed observation of everyday life.

In order to take liberties with drawing, you should first be familiar with drawing itself; in order to simplify, as you must do in cartoons, you should first be familiar with details. One of the basic considerations of good cartooning is learning to differentiate between the essential and the nonessential.

Using a Sketch Book

The use of a sketch book is very important and you should keep it constantly with you. While taking a ride in a bus, for instance, look around at the people sharing the trip with you. Here you find an infinite variety of character, action, expression, and gesture. You can see how clothes hang on people, the relationship between figures and background, lighting and perspective. Make the world your studio, the people in it your models. Sketching is a fine way to keep your work always *alive*.

Your Model

For more sustained study of the model, drawing from the posed figure, in a studio or art school, is recommended. If you cannot get to an art school or sketch class, ask your friends and relatives to pose for you. If a problem of composition or expression stumps you, get somebody to take the pose you need for your cartoon, or pose yourself in front of a mirror. Make a fairly realistic drawing first, and then simplify to fit your cartoon style and composition.

The main things to consider in making a good life drawing are action or gesture, character, and simple form. A mere photographic reproduction of the model will not help you very much in getting a foundation for cartooning. Observe the model from all angles so that you can better portray simple three-dimensional form. Use any medium you can get your hands on. Lead pencil, conte pencil and crayon, and charcoal are good materials to use in sketching from life. However, start working as soon as possible with brush and pen and ink, the two mediums used most extensively in cartoons today.

Experiment as you draw. Make many studies with your pen or brush and ink, without preliminary penciling—a good way to get the practice and eventually feel at home in a reproducible medium. Many sketches should be made of the same pose, the first ones semirealistic, the later ones simpler but more exaggerated in action and character.

Simplicity is the keynote for a good cartoon, but you must be careful not to oversimplify or your cartoons will seem empty and uninteresting. Style is a matter of check and balance, of knowing when you have enough detail and when you have too much.

Creating a Cartoon Style

A cartoon is a stenographic approach to drawing. Getting your idea across *quickly, surely,* and *with humor* is most important. In most cases a too naturalistic portrayal of features, clothes, and background slows down the action of the cartoon. Therefore, we have to create symbols for the whole figure and its various parts.

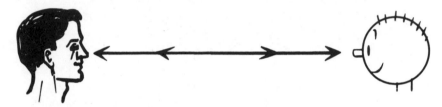

Somewhere between the two extremes shown above lies your particular style of cartoon.

Instead of using a naturalistic head outline, start with a simple abstract shape, such as an oval.

Consider this oval as a piece of wire which may be pulled and stretched into various shapes. As an experiment, take a piece of thin wire, and shape it into a silhouette of a head. Then mold it in various directions. The effects gained will give you a sense of the liberty you have to create outlines and forms.

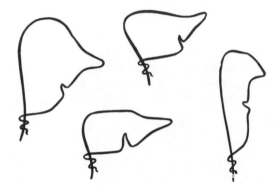

A cartoon style, whether tending towards the abstract (below) or the more realistic (next page), must be based on simple forms.

"You know the rules of the State Wrestling Commission, now get out there and act!"

"I've lost track,
Tim. How many stories we got to go yet?"

THE NEW YORKER

The Features

Take a basic head shape, space certain features within this outline, and you have created a character. Let us start from the top of the head and work down, using our shorthand method.

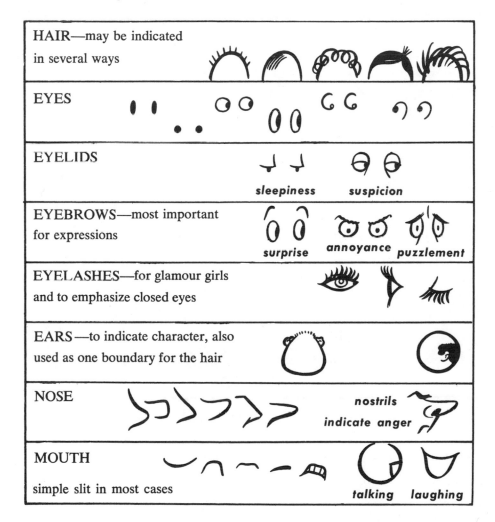

HAIR—may be indicated in several ways

EYES

EYELIDS — *sleepiness* — *suspicion*

EYEBROWS—most important for expressions — *surprise* — *annoyance* — *puzzlement*

EYELASHES—for glamour girls and to emphasize closed eyes

EARS—to indicate character, also used as one boundary for the hair

NOSE — *nostrils indicate anger*

MOUTH — simple slit in most cases — *talking* — *laughing*

Constructing a Complete Head

The drawing of a head outline and a set of features spaced within this shape builds the complete cartoon head. In this example, the portly business tycoon is used as the guinea pig. All drawings should have depth.

Using the abstract shapes below, add a shadow to the side of the head to indicate depth. Place simple features within each face. Remember, the shape of the head and the spacing of the features within this area will create your type.

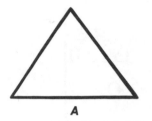 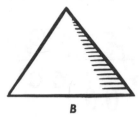 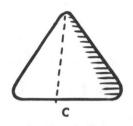

A.   B.   C.

A. Triangle suggests our character.

B. Triangle becomes pyramid when shadow is added, creating three-dimensional form.

C. Pyramid with edges slightly rounded. Dotted line shows center of face, a guide to the placing of features.

A.   B.   C.

A. Addition of nose (a smaller pyramid), eyes, and hair.

B. Eyebrows and moustache added.

C. Complete with bags under eyes, ear, double chin, collar, and tie.

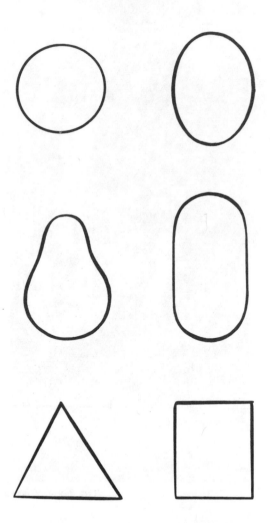

For example, taking the same triangular shape used for the businessman, adding different hair, spacing the eyes closer together and higher in the head, and using a different type of mouth, one which is pushed closer to the other features, we get a large-jawed, tough-guy type.

By inverting the triangle shape and spacing the features lower down, we get more brain room and less jaw space, thereby creating a scholarly type.

SIDE VIEW

Now that we have an idea of the head in three-quarter, let us acquaint ourselves with the head in other positions. The profile or side view is used most frequently in cartoons because of its simplicity (only one eye, one ear, etc., need be indicated). The construction is similar to that of the front or three-quarter view.

For the sake of variety, let us use the pear shape with a slight change of features to get the same tycoon type.

A   B   C

(A) Simple shape with shadow added for depth. (B) Features added. Note closeness of eye to the outline. Moustache extends slightly outside head outline to indicate its thickness. (C) Outline pushed back allowing more brain room.

BACK VIEW

Here, since we do not have too many features to work with, we make the most of the ears and hair.

THREE-QUARTER BACK VIEW

Note eye and moustache outside the outline, ear moved toward front of the face, and hair mass following the rounded form of the head.

In a composition of two figures this view balances a front or three-quarter front view.

Pantomime Cartoon

In a pantomime panel cartoon, which has no caption, the idea is put across primarily by expression and action. Since a multi-panel cartoon usually occupies the same small space in a magazine as a single-panel job, the figures are reproduced quite small. Therefore, as in the example, it sometimes becomes necessary to exaggerate and simplify the features so that the facial expression may be readily seen. In this cartoon the ears were eliminated entirely since they did not especially add to the character or expression of the hunter.

THE SATURDAY EVENING POST

Note the oval-shaped head of the hunter in this picture.

Head Accessories

The moustache and beard may be used with great success for male members of the cast to add variety of character. The moustache may take the place of the mouth entirely, and with it you can indicate many of the same expressions. Eyeglasses may also be used with telling effect to create character and to accent the form of the head.

THE HAT

The hat follows the form of the head whether it is worn properly, tilted, perched on top of the head, or pushed down over the ears. The hat is "meat" for the cartoonist. He has a device here which he can exploit to the fullest to add humor and character to his figures.

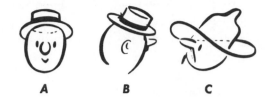

A B C

A. Front view. Hat angled toward back of head.
B. Three-quarter view. Hat tilted forward.
C. Brim drawn in form of figure 8.

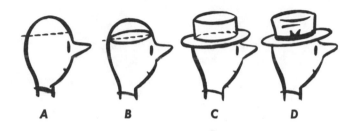

A B C D

A. Angle of hat indicated by broken line.
B. Oval showing how hat goes around head.
C. Basic shape of crown indicated.
D. Varied crown with dents added.

A B C D

A. The cap based on triangular shape.
B. Big hat—small head.
C. Big head—tiny hat.
D. The derby.

Completion of beaten-up hat derived from basic forms.

COLLAR AND TIE

Constructing a Complete Figure

Taking the first head which we constructed, let us build up a figure, complete with arms and legs. Just as you started with a simple shape for the head, indicate a simple form for the body. You again have the choice of an oval, pear shape, square, rectangle, triangle or any other simple shape. You have a triangular head. What body shape will go best with it: triangle, oval, square, rectangle? In this case an oval or pear shape will be the best basis for the body.

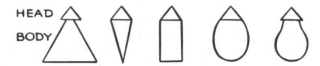

In drawing, *contrast* is most important whether it is contrasting shapes, contrasting lines, or contrasting tones. This helps make a picture interesting to the eye and mind. Therefore—angular head, round body. Also, for the type we are portraying here, the oval is best as a motif for a substantial figure to go with a substantial type.

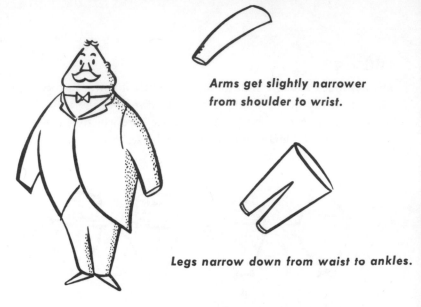

Arms get slightly narrower from shoulder to wrist.

Legs narrow down from waist to ankles.

Get a feeling in your drawing of the lapel going all the way around the head. At this stage, use tubular forms to indicate arms and legs.

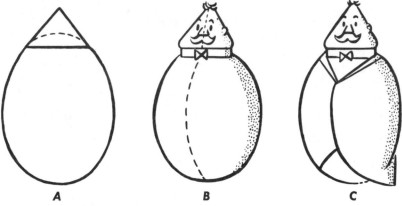

A. **Head superimposed on oval.**

B. **Simple shadow to denote form. Dotted line indicates center of body, a guide to drawing clothes.**

C. **Triangles for lapels. Cutaway coat indicated.**

SIDE VIEW

Even if the figure is in full profile, it is wise to indicate what is happening on the side of the body we cannot see.

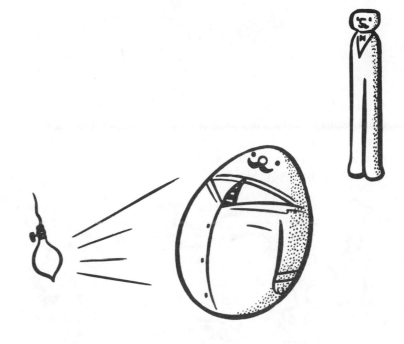

Force an indication of the other arm by showing the left hand and cigar. The left leg adds both dimension and stability to the figure.

BACK VIEW

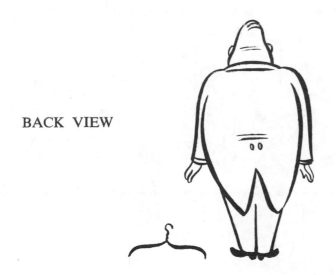

Note coat hanger bulge to express shoulders.

Keep your figures compact, well-knit, and as simple in silhouette as possible. Try this: Raid your icebox and get a hard-boiled egg. When the egg is lighted from one side, observe form and the simplicity of contour. For contrasting shape do the same with a clothespin. Consider the simplicity of these two forms as the basis of cartoon drawing. Draw the head, clothes, and features on the egg and clothespin.

Up to now we have worked with the *static* figure. In a later chapter we will study the figure in action. But first, practice with the static figure, using various body and head shapes in different combinations, rounding out certain parts, and choosing those features you wish to emphasize. The more you practice along these lines, the faster you will develop your own particular cartoon style.

Hands

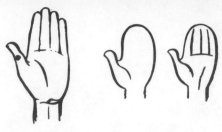

Aside from functioning as a normal part of the human body, hands can be one of the most expressive features in a cartoon. Like everything else in the cartoon, they must be brought down into simple forms. For purposes of modeling at a moment's notice, there are, of course, no hands more readily available than your own.

For simplification, the hand should be thought of as a mitten—the thumb as one unit, and the other four fingers as another whole unit. The wrist should be shown whenever possible. The hand flexing around the wrist will give added action and expression. Remember that when a cartoon is reproduced, the hands show up very small. For this reason, *clarity* is essential.

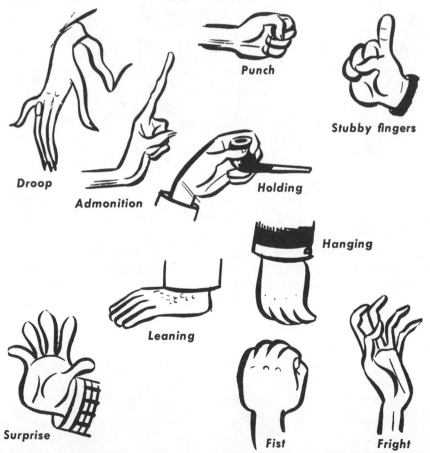

Punch

Stubby fingers

Droop

Admonition

Holding

Hanging

Leaning

Surprise

Fist

Fright

Feet

Feet are primarily used as a base for the body. While feet in a cartoon should not be obtrusive, they can add to the over-all humor of a picture by being flexible. A supple foot will turn at the ankle and the toes. Exaggerate feet more toward smallness than largeness. For example, a mammoth individual with small, mincing feet can be very funny.

THE SATURDAY EVENING POST

An indication of how fluid and supple feet aid in the humor and expression of a cartoon.

Female feet

The bare foot and shoe, side view, may be abstracted down to a triangle.

Again, consider the big toe as one unit, the four smaller toes as another unit.

Three-quarter view

Drawing Cartoon Types

These are some of the leading characters you may have to call upon to help in your production. Your invention may take you from a prison cell to a flying carpet. The cartoonist plays around with an infinite variety of subjects, and he must be ready and able to provide the right character for any setting. There are a tremendous number of types and characters

| Rich man | Poor man | Beggar man | Thief |
| Doctor | Lawyer | Merchant | Chief |

around you ready to be observed, sketched, and filed for future use in your cartoons. However, because the cartoonist covers such a wide field of subjects, there are many types which he would not bump into every day. To name just a few: sultans, harem gals, Foreign Legionnaires, Eskimos, hermits, penguins, Bali beauties, matadors, disk jockeys, lighthouse keepers, and movie directors. Therefore, besides observation and study of the types seen every day, the wise cartoonist studies types which he can only get to know through photographs, movies, television, etc.

Knowing how to draw man in various ages will help you in getting types. Six ages of man will be enough for the cartoonist's purpose—infancy, childhood, youth, manhood, middle age, and old age.

Taking the two extremes, infancy and old age, let us see what characteristics we find in the head profiles.

Both profiles of the baby and the old man may be fitted into a question mark. Both their necks are thin, and both may be bald, but there the resemblance ends.

Head Shapes

The following basic outlines may be used as head shapes for the six age groups:

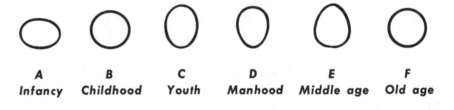

A	B	C	D	E	F
Infancy	*Childhood*	*Youth*	*Manhood*	*Middle age*	*Old age*

The infant's characteristics include the following: eyes below the center line of the head, large forehead, small features, fat cheeks, pouting mouth, everything rounded and full. The old gent's characteristics: smaller forehead, angular lines, face bony and shrunken, hanging folds of skin, scraggly neck. Both the baby's body and the old man's may be bent, but the baby's figure is composed of rounded lines throughout, and his head is quite large for his body. The old man's figure is thin, angular, with thin, bony hands.

Eyes at head center and wide apart; small features usually; thin neck. Right: Eyes below head center and wide apart.

14

C

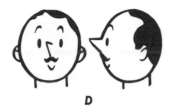

D

Egg-shaped head narrowing towards chin; plenty of hair; eyes slightly above center. Right: Thinning hair; moustache; heavier neck.

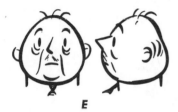

E

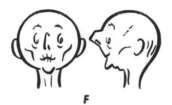

F

Very thin hair; heaviness at base of head; bags under eyes; double chin. Right: Angular; gaunt; sunken features; thin neck.

Girls

The keynote for gals, young or old, is *curves*. For cute girls, curve forehead in. Indicate eyelashes, cute upturned nose, full lips, small mouth, eyes slightly below center of head. In the profile leave sufficient space between the tip of chin and neck. The neck is long, not too thick, and column-like. Oval shapes and curves are also used for the older, more matronly type.

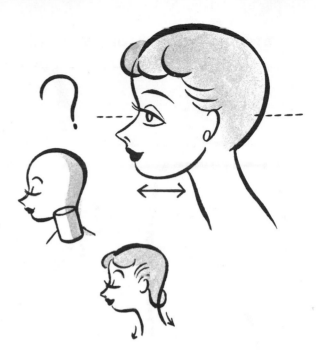

Features are usually smaller than men's.

Heads, front view, are round or heart-shaped, eyes wide apart.

Draw cute girls between 7 and 8 heads high.

There are no set hair-do's or clothes, since styles keep constantly changing.

Thin *waistline is important*.

For the latest fashion, study the gals around you.

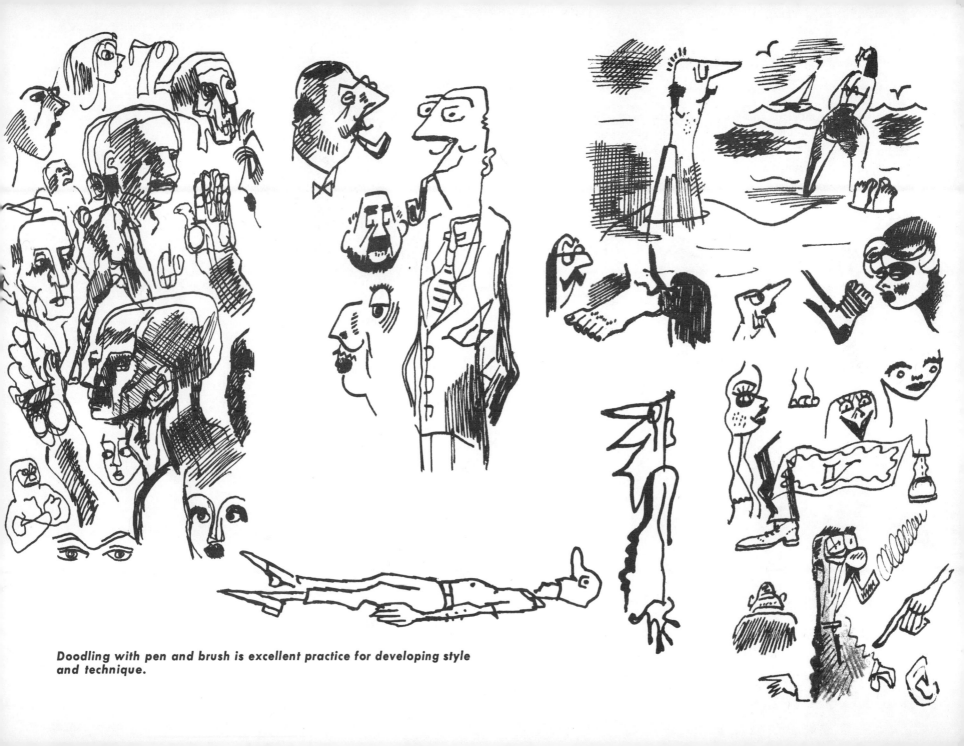

Doodling with pen and brush is excellent practice for developing style and technique.

Animals

Animals are a wonderful addition to your cast of characters. In cartooning animals, observe and emphasize the grace of certain animals, such as the horse, and the heaviness and clumsiness of other animals, such as the elephant. Exaggerated expression conveyed by the eyes and mouth add the comic touch.

Rounded shapes make the pig, flowing lines the horse, angular shapes the cow.

Emotion

You have chosen your characters. Now it is time for them to act out your plot, your cartoon idea. Facial expression, combined with body gesture, is the most important factor in getting your point across with the utmost humor. The humor of the cartoon depends a great deal on the character and expression of the *head*. Faces in cartoons should not be hidden. The greatest impact on the audience will be achieved when the face of the character doing the talking, and the reaction of his remark on the faces of the other players in your cartoon comedy, can be readily seen.

In the following four heads notice how the expression is carried entirely by the movement of the eyebrow and mouth.

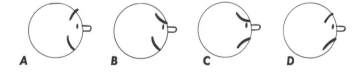

A. Eyebrow and mouth going in opposite directions create a pleased expression.

B. Sardonic look created by eyebrow and mouth both turned up (going in same direction).

C. Eyebrow and mouth turned away from each other convey displeasure.

D. Eyebrow and mouth both in downward direction produce hurt or sad look.

THE AMERICAN LEGION MAGAZINE

Below we show a progression of expression from the faintly amused to the pleased, the quiet laugh, and the guffaw. The movement of the head pivoting at the neck helps build up extreme expression *D*. Also note closed eye in head *D*, to enhance effect.

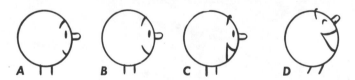

Let us do these in a three-quarter view:

Action of the hair, addition of nostril, and motion lines (head D) also help show extremes of emotion.

Let us now look at varying degrees of anger:

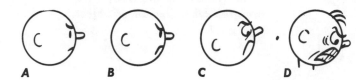

A   B   C   D

In character D we really ham it up, throwing in everything to produce the extreme effect; wrinkles, bags, teeth, nostrils, baleful glare, and a threatening head gesture towards the victim.

Three-quarter view of the Angry One:

Facial expression and body gesture enhance each other.

Three laughing cartoons, showing how action is a factor in extreme expression. Note the slapping hand effect.

Sad character in four stages of emotion:

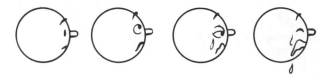

The movement and size of eye are added devices in conveying expression.

 Haughty Coy

Devilish   Modest

The Frightened One:

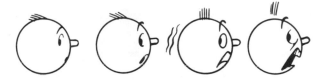

In these expressions of melancholy the body tends to sag downward. The hands also help in conveying emotion—the clenched fist and the drooping fingers.

21

Despondency

Fright-gesture of the body away from the other person or object

Anger-gesture of the body toward the other person or object

Rage

Surprise

Haughtiness-gesture of body upward

Modesty

Here are some more impressions of expressions. Try your own versions of these and others, such as fury, melancholy, surprise, elation, enjoyment, coyness, glee.

Shock

Remorse

Suspicion

Sleepiness

Confidence

Disdain

Poker face

Aggression

Anticipation

Exuberance

Worry

Nobility

Action and Composition

Pose yourself in front of your mirror. Notice how the various parts of your face and body move. A cartoon figure can illustrate all these actions, and more. For, unlike an illustrator, the cartoonist may take extreme liberties in giving life to his cartoon figure—the heads may be twisted entirely around, and the eyes may be popping.

Some cartoon ideas require violent action and some require "quiet" action. Examples of the latter include standing, sitting, talking, the type of action or gesture that is used for quiet, conversational gags.

It is much more difficult to portray a quiet-action cartoon than it is to evolve a violent-action picture of two or three people fighting. The latter is a natural in evoking a reader's interest because of its subject matter and the greater opportunity to exaggerate action lines. In tackling a subject of two people talking, the artist must deal with the action more subtly, since action does not especially aid in putting this type of cartoon idea across.

Most beginning students make a common error when composing two figures together; their first efforts have a sameness of posture, and the result is monotony.

This is a little better. By curving one of the figures we get a more interesting picture. Already, tension is beginning to develop between the two main elements of the picture. But this is not enough. Drawing both figures in profile still makes for monotony.

A three-quarter front view and a three-quarter back view add still more interest. One thin figure and one heavier figure create more variety of character.

A table or desk connecting the figures help solidify the composition.

Another improvement would be to have one figure standing and one seated.

Why do we try to avoid straight up and down lines as the basis for our figures? Why do we prefer lines such as these?

One good reason is that backgrounds, props, furniture, wall panels, doors, and windows must be drawn, in most cases, with horizontal or vertical lines. Therefore, whenever possible, you are *obliged* to use a different type of line as the basis for your figures in order to relieve the monotony of these horizontal or vertical prop and background lines. Also, curved, diagonal, or dynamic lines used as a basis for your figures will, by their contrast with the more monotonous background lines, draw the reader's attention to the figures. This is as it should be, since people are the most important element in any cartoon.

Remember, these are static lines.   **These are active, dynamic lines.**

Observe the direction and contrast of line in the following illustrations.

Hooked line of the figure contrasting with straight lines of structures.

Streamlined action line gives speed to the baker and contrasts with straight lines of the building and the engine.

Violent Action

Observe the running gentleman below. All the devices to provide speed are used and the entire figure is based on a streamline. The hair, necktie, coattails, glasses, and hat fly back, accentuating the pushing, forward motion of the figure. Speed lines are used and the figure gains more action by being lifted off the ground.

What is your version of a running figure? In cartooning there are no set action poses. You have complete liberty to twist, stretch, and turn your figures to get proper action and to make your brainchildren silly and funny looking. In drawing an active character, begin with a simple stick figure emphasizing the big line of action. By doing this you completely concentrate on the action first. Later, you may build up the figure however you wish—fat, thin, old, young, etc.

The body bent back results in an unorthodox running posture which, by its departure from the normal running position, adds humor to the figure.

A speedier runner.

More extreme action line, resulting in the speediest runner of all.

Walking

Graceful fall

Awkward fall

Three-point landing

Kicking

Back kick

Balancing

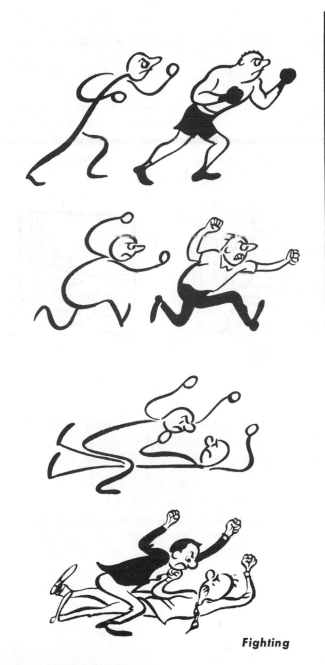

Running

Jumping

Fighting

Diving

Walking

27

Drawing Backgrounds

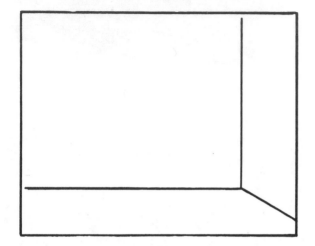

Every object, no matter how complex, can be broken down into basic, simple forms. Once you have done that, you can begin to add detail. Thus, a living room can be seen as the inside of a cube. Add windows,

a door, lamps, drapes, etc., and you have the start of a picture pleasing to the eye.

Draw your own room for practice. First, put down the bare skeleton of the room, or corner of the room. Then embroider it with windows, doors, pictures, and lighting fixtures. Windows and door are much used props in cartoons. Indicate thickness in these, as in all other props. Practice drawing doors open, shut, and partly open.

Interiors

Draw these props carefully at first, *even using a ruler,* until you get to the point where you can draw them casually and simply, retaining the big aspects of the prop without obtruding upon the more important living characters in the picture.

Observe interiors wherever you go. They may come in handy in future cartoons you draw. Also, observe interiors in movies and television productions as well as those in magazine photographs, for a cartoonist is called upon to draw many unfamiliar interiors, ranging from the interior of a harem to that of a prison cell. Knowledge of chandeliers and where to put them is important in pinning down the character of a room, as well as adding height to a picture.

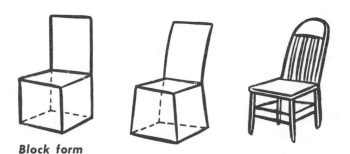

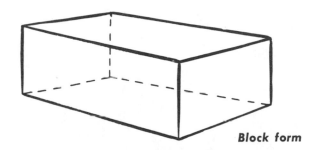

Block form

Curtains and drapes require study and simplification of folds. Rugs are important for the design quality and texture that they add to a picture. Similarly, practice on radiators, venetian blinds, or anything that dresses up the walls, ceiling, and floor of a room.

Block form

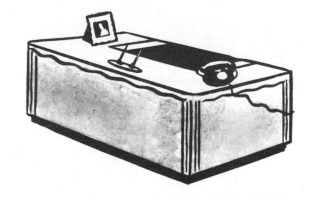

Block form

Getting away from the walls and into the room, we have the problem of furniture. Again, valuable research may be done directly in your own rooms and in pictures in mail-order catalogs and furniture ads. As you introduce furniture into your picture, start again with a simple, solid shape. Then add details and ornamentation.

29

Grass

Outdoors

Take a stroll around your neighborhood. Fill your sketch book with typical outdoor gimmicks—lamp posts, store windows, bus-stop signs, hydrants, letter boxes, bushes, hedges, trees. Unlike most indoor props such as walls, doors, and windows, which are rigid, you will find many outdoor props which may be twisted and turned to suit your design and composition. Trees, clouds, and hills offer such opportunities for fluidity. There is no set pose for these objects, and judicious use may be made of their plasticity to make a cartoon composition more interesting. How simply can you transcribe them?

Tree bent

to frame composition

Textures also play a great part in making your props, and eventually your composition, easy to look at. Note that texture is merely decoration. Don't lose the form of an object by letting textures get in the way. In inking, the outlines of the tree and the house would be rendered in

strong lines. Tree bark, siding shingle, and brick textures should be rendered in lighter lines so that they are completely enclosed in the bigger form. Otherwise, they will jump out at you and take interest away from the more important object in the picture.

Technique

The principal techniques used today in cartooning are *line* and *half-tone*. Color is also being used more and more in magazine cartoons. Whether your cartoon ends up as a line drawing or a half-tone drawing, the elements of your picture, in most cases, have to be outlined in brush and ink or pen and ink. This outline is the basis of your cartoon. Thereafter, solid blacks and textural effects may be added to complete a line drawing, wash or rubbed tone added to complete a half-tone drawing, or color added to complete a color cartoon.

Line Reproduction

Line drawing is the most direct way of working a cartoon. It reproduces clearly and inexpensively, and it is the best technique for newspaper work and for reproduction on cheaper grades of paper. Although a line drawing doesn't have the depth and atmosphere of a half-tone, there are many ways to make a line drawing interesting.

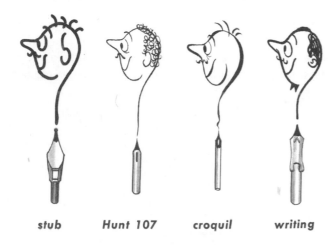

stub   Hunt 107   croquil   writing

You may eventually become either a pen-and-ink artist or a brush-and-ink artist, but give both the pen and the brush a good try before deciding which is better suited for you. Go to a stationery or art-supply store and buy yourself about a dozen different kinds of pen points. It is not enough to have some artists' drawing pen points. Ordinary writing pen points are valuable, too, in cartooning.

flowing line   nervous line   broken line

Doodle constantly with this variety of points. Get the feel of the pen. By experimenting with various pen points you will soon hit upon the point or points best suited to your individual needs. You may like to use a croquil pen point, which is flexible, or an ordinary writing point, which will give you a strong, even line. The idea is to get a line heavy enough to reproduce well. The smoother, or plate-finish, Bristol board is fine for pen work.

THE SATURDAY EVENING POST

"The captain says come up—the ship is sinking."

A studied, decorative line was used here, gliding from thin to thick and back again to thin. You may also use a more slashy, looser brush line in cartoons, or an even line all around. Occasionally you may use a dry brush line, which is obtained by dipping the brush into the ink, partly

31

drying off the brush by making a few brush strokes on a piece of scrap paper or blotter, and then applying the brush to your drawing.

Whether you use a pen or brush, these are the elements that will make your drawing more interesting:

White of paper   **Solid black**   **Variety of line textures**

In separate pans, mix three separate tones of wash.

light   *medium*   *dark*

With the white of the paper and the solid black of the India ink you now have five tones, which should be sufficient for the average cartoon.

Wash Half-tone

Materials necessary are the following:

Good paper heavy enough to take repeated washes without buckling. A grained or kid-finish paper is best.

Three- or four-ply Bristol board or illustration board will take wash well.

Charcoal gray, lamp black, or ivory black in water color tubes of good grade.

Black India ink diluted with water will also give some good wash tones.

Two or three fairly large brushes; at least one number 4 brush for smaller areas, and one number 7 brush for larger areas.

Don't hamper yourself by using inferior materials. Good materials mean that your work may be done more easily, more quickly, and more economically. A fine grade of brush used for water color will last for many years. Good illustration and Bristol boards may be cut into fours, reducing the cost of each drawing considerably.

Apply wash to your outlined cartoon. A good strong line goes well with washes. The light tone is usually used for simple modeling on faces, hands, and light objects The medium and darker tones are used on clothes and darker objects. For easy handling, apply wash, in order, to each small section of the drawing bounded by black outlines. In the cartoon above, section No. 1 was washed in first, then section No. 2, then section No. 3. Should a puddle form on the drawing at the completion of a wash, dry your brush on a rag, and with the dried brush lift up the excess water to flatten your tone.

Rubbed Tone

Rub the conte stick over a sandpaper block, creating pencil dust.

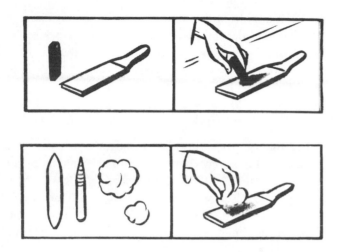

For rubbed tones, use No. 2 black conte stick and sandpaper block.

Rubbed tone reproduces about the same as wash, and is easier to handle and control. You can make changes and erasures quite easily, lay down flat tones over large areas, and obtain interesting textural effects.

Rub paper stumps (available in art stores) or absorbent cotton over the pencil dust on the sandpaper block. The paper stumps or cotton can then be applied to the drawing paper.

Whites picked out with a pointed, kneaded eraser

Use larger wad of cotton for larger areas, smaller wads and stumps for smaller areas. Tones once put down on paper may be lightened by rubbing a piece of *clean* cotton over them. Tones that don't satisfy may be entirely erased (with a kneaded eraser) and a new tone applied.

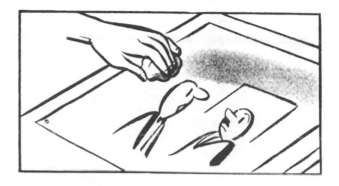

EXAMPLES OF DRAWINGS FOR HALF-TONE REPRODUCTION

Rubbed tone

"From now on Ulag-18 will review the books on interplanetary travel."

THE NEW YORK TIMES BOOK REVIEW

"Maybe I shouldn't have given him all those 'How to' books."

Creating Cartoon Ideas

With patience and hard work, almost anyone can develop the ability to originate humor for cartoon panels. Good salable gags do not come easily even to the most accomplished idea men. Nowadays, the regular weekly routine of the cartoonist is, first, the invention of from 10 to 20 fresh humorous situations, and then the presentation of these ideas in sketch form to the various cartoon editors. Some good funny lines are garnered from chance conversation, or remarks overheard, but the number of these is only a small percentage of a cartoonist's annual total of cartoon roughs. An idea may begin with either the caption or the picture. Inspiration comes mostly in the quiet seclusion of the cartoonist's work room. Here, toiling alone and using visual and other aids as stimuli, he can cover a wide range of subjects.

The gag idea is all-important in selling a cartoon. While editors will buy a comic with a funny idea but with only adequate drawing, the finest drawing coupled with a poor gag will never sell. For the complete effectiveness of a cartoon, the idea and the drawing should be equally excellent. Many a funny gag, however, has been completely slaughtered by the novice who did not know how to put his idea across. Fortunate is the cartoonist who can both draw well and originate fine gags.

Categories of cartoonists at work today include: 1. those who create all their own ideas; 2. those who create some of the gags and buy some from professional gagmen; 3. those who purchase *all* ideas from gagmen. There are some cartoonists who have no flair at all for dreaming up funny ideas. These cartoonists need not despair. They should concentrate on their drawing, building up a humorous, unique style, and they will soon find gagmen with whom they can collaborate on ideas and captions. Some publications like *The New Yorker* and *Playboy* will buy and provide ideas for those artists who have a talent for humorous drawing. At any rate, competent comic draftsmen can always obtain work in the ever-widening field of cartoon advertising and comic illustration for magazines and books.

Here are several types of gags that cartoonists originate, and the devices for turning these gags into humorous, completed cartoons.

Surprise Ending Picture

Multi-panel pantomime cartoons are always popular with editors and usually command higher prices. They vary from two to six or eight panels. The first panels are played "straight." The surprise, the unexpected, takes place in the very last panel. In thinking up his idea the cartoonist usually visualizes the last panel first. He then builds up his continuity in the first panels to lead to that big bang at the end.

Make your own collection of this type of cartoon from newspapers and magazines. Then, cover the last, the surprise panel. Study the first panels and see if you can think of another ending, one that will top the original.

"I've been asked to get married twelve times—all by my father."

With this same picture, you could very easily use other captions such as, "The only thing standing in the way of my getting a divorce is I'm not married to him yet."

Reverse Gag

This is a reverse of the usual situation of Easterners reading Westerns. This type of gag is used a great deal in magazines.

THIS WEEK MAGAZINE

Surprise Ending Caption

This is purely a conversational type of gag. The gag line is all-important. The picture merely establishes the characters and setting. The first part of the caption starts conventionally enough; the latter part of the same conversation piece contains the twist, the surprise.

THE NEW YORK TIMES BOOK REVIEW

"I'm gittin' bored, Tex. Got any good 'Easterns'?"

Another reverse gag in three-panel form. Boy hits top hat. Top hat hits boy. This cartoon also combines the qualities of a gadget gag, a cliché picture gag, and a surprise ending gag.

THE SATURDAY EVENING POST

Cliché Picture

You've seen hundreds of cartoons on these subjects, and you will see many hundreds more in the future. Despite the fact that these items have been run into the ground, editors will always buy picture clichés if a *good, new, fresh* variation on the theme is presented. Magazines use them continually.

Some of the clichés in *picture* form are as follows:

Note in milk bottle	Ladder—two people eloping
Man reading eye chart	Operating theater of hospital
Crystal gazer	Father playing with son's toys
Tunnel of love	Neighbor borrowing cup of sugar
Desert island	Woman being fitted for shoes
Bed of nails	Diner annoyed at slowness of waiter

REPRINTED BY PERMISSION OF COSMOPOLITAN MAGAZINE

Cartoon based on eye chart

The idea for the cartoon based on the eye chart was evolved by first studying the normal eye chart situation. Then followed concentration on the eye chart itself—trying to think of something to replace the varied-size letters. Musical notes finally came to mind as a substitute for the usual printed letters on the chart.

Cliché Caption

Gags based on clichés always have good sales value. True, these expressions are old, but a good, fresh, surprising picture coupled with that familiar remark will produce a funny cartoon.

First, make up a list of clichés for study. These may be culled from conversations overheard, radio and television programs, books or newspapers.

"Listen, Helen. They're playing our song."

Other versions of the same cliché as the one shown above:

Snake charmer playing his instrument, two snakes emerging from basket.

One snake to the other, "Listen, dear, he's playing our song." Stout couple lounging in deck chairs. Ship's steward ringing dinner chimes.

Portly man to wife, "Listen, darling—he's playing our song!"

These clichés may be used in their original form, or changed slightly.

"Try this one for size."
"Everything's in ship-shape order."
"Go away and never darken my door again."
"Woman's work is never done."
"Mind if I look over your shoulder while you work?"
"Don't keep me in the dark."
"It isn't polite to point."
"I'm a stranger in town myself."
"You should have seen the one that got away."
"He's in conference."
"Having a wonderful time, wish you were here."
"We're just made for each other."

The Gadget Gag

You can develop a gadget gag by studying props and observing how they work. Pictures in mail-order catalogs, photographs and drawings of furniture, household appliances, and other props are studied by the

THE NEW YORKER

cartoonist, and a logical misuse is found for them as a basis of cartoon ideas. The shape, the size, the movement, and the relation of these props to human beings are studied. This is a real *visual* aid to gag making.

For instance, musical instruments are funny-looking objects just as they are, and when put to work in a way never intended by musical-instrument manufacturers, laughs will result. We have trombones with slides, music stands which can be raised and lowered, cymbals which bang together, drums which look like tables or soup tureens, horns with intestine-like coils, violins that nestle under the chin, xylophones which resemble ironing boards, and harps which look like bed springs. In addition, the musicians playing these instruments look so serious when performing that we have ample material here for satirical drawing.

Gags Based on Signs

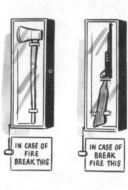

In this cartoon the literal use of the sign brings forth the gag.

TRUE

THE SATURDAY EVENING POST

"He has a one hundred and sixty-eight bar rest."

Here the usual sign is given a reverse twist.

38

General Subjects

General subjects like sports, theater, office, and home are good at all times. When trying to get inspiration from any subject, break it down into small categories. For instance, subheadings under "office" can be water cooler, dictaphone, desk, suggestion box, business chart, lettering on office door, filing cabinet. Concentrate on one item for quite a while and you will find ideas developing.

NATION'S BUSINESS

"Yes, J. T., business is a great thing. Why I've arranged some of my best foursomes right in my office."

magazines, the ones that pay the highest prices for cartoons, are circulated all over the country. Your subject matter must be familiar to all these people; otherwise your gag idea will fall flat. For this reason gags on the mere process of living (so familiar to everyone) are the ones most used by magazines. That is why home gags are so popular—gags based on the simple daily things we do from dressing in the morning, washing, brushing our teeth, to transportation home from the office in the evening, eating, reading the newspaper, listening to the radio, watching TV—and so to bed.

THE SATURDAY EVENING POST

In conclusion, the most important point is this: *your subject matter must be understandable and familiar to almost everybody*. Avoid specialized subjects or private jokes (unless you are dealing with specialized magazines such as trade publications). Remember, the mass circulation

From Rough to Finish

The professional cartoonist submits from eight to twenty ideas a week in sketch form for acceptance by the cartoon editors of various publications. These sketches are called *cartoon roughs*. Since the artist at this point is working purely on speculation, the submission of sketches instead of finished drawings is a great time-saving device.

Most cartoonists prepare their sketches on a standard size bond typewriting paper, 8½ by 11″. This size assures ease of handling by the editor, and the roughs may be mailed in standard-size manila envelopes, thus saving time and labor. White paper is most commonly used, although colored stock is used by some cartoonists. Bond paper is inexpensive and may be bought by the ream. A durable paper with some rag content, of at least a twenty-pound weight, should be chosen. This will be heavy enough to withstand punishment in mailing and handling, transparent enough to be traced through with or without a light box, and lightweight enough to keep your mailing bill down. For those cartoonists who like to prepare their sketches in wash techniques, a heavier weight than twenty-pound is recommended to insure against buckling of the paper.

Preparing the Rough

You may use your 8½ by 11″ paper either horizontally or vertically in preparing your rough. However, stick to one or the other in any particular batch of sketches. Remember, the editor runs through as many as 1000 sketches on a cartoon "look" day. Make it as easy as possible for him to judge your work. If he has to twist and turn the roughs in your batch from the horizontal to the vertical, and back again, your work will be at a slight disadvantage. Even if you are a "vertical rough" man, certain subjects may call for a horizontal rough or two, but let this mixture be the exception rather than the rule. Should you typewrite your captions, you will find that the vertical way of working is best, since typewriting paper in a horizontal position does not fit into the standard typewriter. However, many cartoonists find it easier to compose pictures on paper held horizontally, and on these roughs the captions will have to be hand lettered. Your rough is your best salesman. *It,* and *it alone,* will sell your work.

For a horizontal rough, allow about 1″ white space at the top and sides and 2″ at the bottom.

Roughs may be rendered in any technique that comes easiest and fastest to the cartoonist. Soft pencil, pen and ink, brush and ink, black wash, blue wash, and even color (water color or crayon) may be used—anything that you can use with confidence and that will make the work presentable. The professional cartoonist whose finished work is known to the editor can do a very rough rough. However, the beginning cartoonist should do as finished a sketch as he can. This will familiarize the editor with his capabilities in doing reproducible work. It will also provide the novice with constant practice in precise drawing. Many a magazine today will reproduce a cartoon directly from the rough, thus eliminating the necessity for the artist to do a more finished drawing. Therefore, some cartoonists render their sketches in black and white with brush or pen and ink fit for direct reproduction from the rough.

Your entire batch of roughs should be consistent in size, in spacing, in technique, and in the handling of the caption. For example, if you render one rough in brush and ink, keep your entire batch in brush and ink. If you decide on typing your captions, stick to the typewriter all through your batch.

For a vertical rough, leave at least 1″ white space on sides, 1¼″ on top, and 2¾″ at the bottom. The cartoon unit may be a square shape or a shape slightly higher than wide. White space around the picture is necessary to isolate it in one spot, so that it will be easily seen and grasped. The caption should be a compact unit under the picture with white space around it.

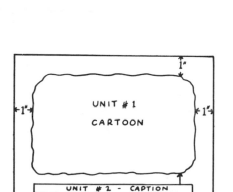

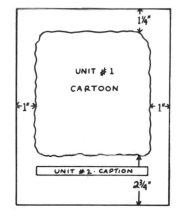

The Caption

The caption should be presented in a clear manner, easily legible. Typing is best for the caption. Otherwise, you will have to resort to hand-lettering either in pencil or ink. In the hand-lettered caption a neat, simple style of letter should be used. A style of lettering similar to the balloon type used in comic strips is good. Lettering may be done in all upper case or a combination of upper and lower case.

Here is a time-saving device which will insure consistency of size and layout in lettering on roughs:

On a piece of blank bond paper rule 4 lines with a ruling pen as shown. This is your master lettering sheet.

When ready to letter captions, place roughs in turn over this sheet, keeping edges of the two sheets even. Your ruled lines will show through

enough and act as guide lines when you lay out your lettering on your rough.

Many artists prefer to letter their captions in pencil so that if a last-minute change in the caption is required, a simple erasure will do the trick. A 3B pencil is recommended for this, black enough so that the caption may be easily seen, but not too soft to be easily smudged. Pen

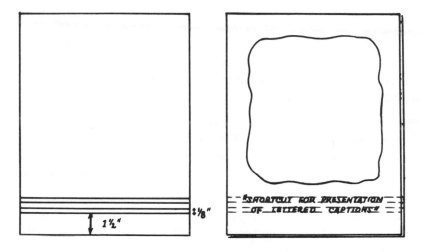

and India ink, or a fountain pen containing a good black ink, is recommended for the inked caption. A final word about captions—watch your punctuation, place quotation marks in the right places, and *be careful of spelling.*

Your rough, whether sketchy or more finished, should get your idea across directly. What you are getting at should be grasped easily and quickly by the editor. The main actors in your setting should be clearly defined, the type of setting clearly indicated.

Your name and address should be placed on the *back* of every rough. A rubber stamp is a great time-saver for this purpose.

The Finished Cartoon

Comes the happy day when you hold clutched in your hand a rough with a nice big OK stamped across the top. "How near to my rough should my finished drawing be?" will probably be your next question.

Unless a definite size and proportion are indicated by the editor, you may stick pretty close to the proportions of your rough. Magazines like the *Saturday Evening Post* and *True* require no set sizes for finished drawings. Just be careful not to make your drawing too tall, since a reduction of the drawing down to its standard 4" width will give the cartoon too much height, and will take up too much space on the magazine page. A good proportion for these magazines is 4" wide and not more than 4" high in the reproduction.

Newspapers confine you to line drawings, but in most magazines the medium is left to the discretion of the artist. You will find the line treatment good for simple subjects and for multi-panel cartoons. A half-tone treatment is excellent for more elaborate subjects, such as the portrayal of crowds.

The contents of the cartoon itself should not be changed too much from rough to finish. The elements that have helped sell your cartoon are its humor, characterization, and effectiveness of idea. Perhaps a detail like the expression on a certain character's face has greatly aided in the sale. Retain it. Many a finished drawing has had to be redone because the artist was too ambitious in transferring his impressions from rough to finish. In many cases roughs are fresh in characterization and direct in composition. *Keep these qualities in your finished drawing.* You must retain the main impact, while possibly improving quality of line, lighting, background details, decoration, and texture. This is, of course, an individual matter. Cartoonists who do scrawly roughs may have to start from scratch in doing the finish. Cartoonists with finished roughs need only trace the outlines of their roughs and add detail where necessary. In most cases a piece of tracing paper need only be placed over the rough, the general contours of the drawing traced and refined here and there as you go along. Do not trace your outlines as you would a map. Keep your drawing flexible in its transfer from rough to finish. Try to recapture the spirit of the drawing, using the rough as a general basis for an improved drawing. When tracing is completed, transfer to your Bristol or illustration board, and apply your technique. Leave white space around your drawing. The caption should then be lettered in *blue pencil* underneath the finished drawing.

The OK

"If there's a shortage of teachers, I haven't noticed it."

42

The rough sketch

"If there's a shortage of teachers, I haven't noticed it."

SATURDAY REVIEW

The finished drawing

Selling

More and more publications, large and small, are using cartoons. The field is tremendous. Trade papers, house organs, as well as the large national magazines, are avid for good gag cartoons. In this field the newcomer is generally encouraged. Lists and trends of cartoon markets are available in several trade publications directed to the cartoonist. The *Writer's Digest Year Book* lists, in detail, markets, cartoon editors, prices, and magazine requirements. In a special department for cartoonists, each monthly issue of *Writer's Digest* contains current news and latest developments in cartoon buying. Special volumes listing thousands of trade journals and house organs may be purchased or are available at the public libraries. These are current users and potential buyers of panel cartoons.

Which Magazine?

Prices of magazine cartoons range from $10 to around $100 depending on the size, circulation, and importance of the publication. There are quite a few $50 to $100 markets. Naturally, most cartoonists aim at the higher paying, mass-circulation magazines and newspapers. These are fine showcases where the cartoon will be seen by millions of readers. Before taking your portfolio of cartoons on the road, study these publications to determine where to submit what. You will notice that some magazines, such as *McCall's, Redbook, Better Homes and Gardens, Ladies' Home Journal,* use family cartoons, centered mostly about the home. Some publications will use a great many cartoons about children. Some will use a broad type of humor, others a quieter gag.

There are many magazines for men which use only such subjects as hunting, fishing, football, baseball, and other sports, as well as subjects which point up male supremacy. Some magazines will go in heavily for captionless or multiple panel cartoons. Others will lean towards the conversational gag.

When to Show

Cartoon roughs may be submitted in person or mailed to cartoon editors. In New York, Wednesday is the day when the editors look at cartoons. Some magazines, particularly the weeklies, "look" every week; the monthlies consider work every two weeks or every month. Be able to navigate quickly from one editorial office to another, and you will find yourself covering many markets in one day. Often, editors may comment on certain roughs and recommend changes which may lead to a sale.

Selling by Mail

For those who do not live in or near New York City or other large cities where magazines are published, selling by mail is a necessity. The post office is the ace salesman for many cartoonists.

In sending to editors:

1. Mail your 8½ by 11″ roughs in 9 × 12″ manila envelopes.
2. Enclose corrugated board or other backing to protect the roughs.
3. Enclose self-addressed stamped envelope (9 × 12″ folded) to insure proper return.
4. No letter or note to the editor is necessary with your submission. If you write a letter, you will have to mail first class. First-class mail is faster, but much more expensive.
5. Third-class mail does the trick, and is less expensive. Do not seal third-class mail packages.
6. Keep track of each batch you send out. Keep a list of the roughs in each envelope you send out, and check off those that come back, to determine what the editor is holding for future consideration.

7. A rubber stamp with your name and address is essential for every cartoonist. Use this on the back of roughs, and also as a return address indication on manila envelopes.

Related Fields

Producing gag drawings, whether in rough or finished form, will give you a good workout, excellent training, and a fine foundation for other fields. Regular production of eight or ten fairly finished roughs a week will give you the knowledge of techniques, ease of brush or pen and ink work, the facility which you can use elsewhere. Many cartoonists, having gone through the mill of several years of gag cartoon work, are now doing successful syndicated strips and panels.

Gag cartooning is an entirely speculative profession. However, if you can pick up other work, such as doing humorous spots, humorous illustration, caricature, greeting cards, cartoon advertising, and television cartoons, you will be assured of security. Some cartoonists have regular "accounts" lasting five or ten years or longer, doing cartoon spots for established departments in weekly or monthly magazines. Other cartoonists have picked up advertising campaigns which run for several years and which assure them a regular yearly income. It pays to keep many irons in the fire.

Advertising Cartoons

Advertising cartoons bring the most money of all. Although well-known cartoonists are picked by advertising agencies to illustrate their copy, the field is open to the not-so-well-known cartoonist. Here, versatility is a great asset. Pen, brush, line, half-tone, two-color, and full-color cartoons are used for trade paper ads, slick magazine ads, car cards, posters, and direct mail folders.

A variety of techniques should be displayed in your sample book. Advertising cartoon drawing, in most cases, is more restricted than gag cartoon drawing. Quality of line and technique are important. The characters depicted must be in most cases well-to-do middle-class people with good clothes, nice cars, and nice homes.

Read some published ads and illustrate the copy for your samples. Telephone or write advertising agencies, get the names of the art directors (the larger agencies have several art directors, each handling certain accounts), and show your wares, either in person or by mailing in samples. Assignments are given out in the form of layouts. In these layouts everything is all set for you, even in most cases the idea. *Your job is to interpret the art director's sketch in your own style and technique.*

Caricature

In caricature, likeness, humor, and simplicity are all-important. Caricatures are usually done on assignment for newspapers and magazines.

Humorous Illustration

To do humorous illustrating for stories or articles, present your sample book personally to the art editor after telephoning for an appointment, or mail samples if you live out of town. If the art editor likes your work, a manuscript will be given to you for illustration. When an assignment is given to the artist, the art editor will indicate size and method of reproduction (line, half-tone, color, etc.) to be used.

Since important story and article copy is illustrated by the use of larger drawings, examples of more elaborate work must be shown to the art

director. These samples may be made by first reading some published stories or articles by humorists such as S. J. Perelman, Damon Runyon, Mark Twain, selecting a few high spots in these writings and converting them into pictures. Often, published gag drawings make acceptable samples.

Comic Strips and Panels

Syndicates are always on the lookout for new features. Submit two weeks' finished work based on sizes of strips or panels found in your local paper.

Editor and Publishers Syndicate Directory lists all the current features, the artist's name, and the syndicate which distributes them. It is a handy book to have if you are trying to sell a feature.

Cartoon Spots

Cartoon spots are used as decorations on a page to break up the monotony of a page full of type. Since spots are reproduced quite small—in some cases about the size of a postage stamp—essential factors are clarity of line, simplicity of design, and blacks well distributed. You may cash in on your spot drawing ability in two ways:

THE NEW YORKER

45

SPOTS ON SPECULATION

Choose a publication that uses spot drawings, study its format carefully, and do a series of spots which you think will be acceptable to this magazine. For example, the spots on this page were drawn for *The New Yorker*. These drawings were made after the artist had observed the type of magazine, the fact that spots are used in this magazine to head its departments, and the size and proportion of the spots used. Besides department heading decorations, many publications print column filler spots, and, sometimes, spots placed in the middle of a page. The main characteristic of these decorative drawings is the pictorial quality; they

THE NEW YORKER

THE NEW YORKER

should contain some idea, but the idea need not be as strong as that of a gag cartoon. Subject matter is important. Seasonal pictures—Christmas, Halloween, Spring, Thanksgiving, etc.—are always in demand. Spots on the subjects of medicine, aviation, railroads, and other specialties may find a home in magazines in those fields. They may also be used to illustrate books.

THE NEW YORKER

SPOTS ON ORDER

Make up a presentation book containing examples of your work—some reproduced spots (category above) which you have sold on speculation, or spot drawings which you have done especially for this sample book. This book is shown to art editors of various magazines, and on the basis of this, definite assignments are often given to the artist to illustrate articles, columns, and stories. Artists who live far from large publishing centers and so are unable to see art buyers, sometimes design and print a mailing piece, a brochure displaying their wares, which is sent to editors. This is a very useful procedure, also, in making your work known to advertising agency art buyers.

Greeting Cards

This is a vast field which ties in neatly with the business of thinking up and drawing funny pictures. Sketches for studio cards may be done in pencil, ink, and/or color. Submissions are mailed to the many card houses with the usual stamped, return-address envelope. Some firms, having their own large art staffs to render finished work, buy ideas only, for which they pay well. Other companies buy both the gag and the finished art from the free lancer. A free-lance market list may be obtained by writing to The Greeting Card Association, 30 Rockefeller Plaza, New York City, 10020.

Christmas cards may be planned for various sizes. Some popular shapes are 6⅛ by 4¾"; 3¼ by 8½"; and 4¼ by 8⅛"—used either horizontally or vertically. It is usually best to show sketches in these sizes, although sketches may be also submitted on 8½ by 11" paper. The idea and design in most cases, is carried only on the front of the card—with a conventional greeting in type on the inside. One exception is the studio type of Christmas card where the idea and picture are carried to the inside fold. Pencil, pen, or brush and ink, with added color is best for rendition of sketches. Christmas card companies work well ahead of time; designs are usually bought one to two years before publication.

For *Studio Cards,* the usual set size is 3¾" wide by 8½" high. Once you are on a card company's mailing list, you will receive regular notices of its current needs. These firms buy a great variety of subjects—anniversary, birthday, get well, travel, St. Valentine's Day, to name just a few. The few giant companies have their own large art departments and usually buy only ideas from freelancers. The medium and small firms buy both art and ideas. Sketches may be submitted in any medium—pencil alone, ink, or color. Bear in mind that the idea and picture start on the front of the folded card (page 1) and are carried forward and completed on the inside, either across pages 2 and 3 or, most usually, on page 3.

Sketches are submitted by mail with the usual self-addressed, stamped return envelope. When the card is OK'd, the artist then makes the finished drawings in black and white—as many drawings as there are colors on the sketch. The drawing for the blacks used (called the key plate) is done on bristol or illustration board. Drawings for the other colors used (red, yellow, etc.) are also done in black ink on separate sheets of acetate (heavy tracing paper) placed in turn over the key drawing. Art directors of card companies will send you explicit directions on this when the OK time comes.

The card shown on this page has been a best seller for D. Forer and Company, Inc.

Jack Markow, a practicing cartoonist for many years, has had thousands of cartoons published in leading magazines here and abroad.

He studied drawing, print making and painting at the Art Students League under Boardman Robinson and Richard Lahey and at the Académie Moderne in Paris under Jean Marchand. He sold his first cartoon to *The New Yorker,* and since then his work has appeared in many publications, including *The Saturday Evening Post, This Week Magazine, Ladies' Home Journal, Holiday,* The New York *Times Magazine* and *Book Review, Argosy, True, Sports Illustrated, Redbook Magazine, McCall's Magazine, Cosmopolitan, Nation's Business* and Canada's *Weekend Magazine.* His work has been reproduced in many cartoon collections, including Thomas Craven's *Cartoon Cavalcade* and all editions of *Best Cartoons of the Year.*

He has done cartoon ads for such accounts as Tydol Gasoline, Post Toasties, Pepsi-Cola, Parker Pen, Marlin Blades, Dentyne Gum, Bond Bread, Kelly Tires, Bacardi Rum, Angostura Bitters, and Metro-Goldwyn-Mayer.

As a painter and print maker, he has exhibited in many leading galleries and museums in this country, and he has had three one-man shows in New York City. His work is found in the permanent collections of the Metropolitan Museum, Hunter College, City College, Brooklyn Museum, University of Georgia, and others.

Mr. Markow's varied experience includes several years as Cartoon Editor of *Argosy* magazine and originator of the course in magazine cartooning at the School of Visual Arts, New York, where he taught for eight years. Many of his students are now prominent in the magazine and syndicate cartooning fields. He also writes a monthly column, "Cartoonist Q's," for *Writer's Digest.*